How *Hamilton* Made It to the Stage

Gerry Boehme

Cavendish Square

New York

Published in 2019 by Cavendish Square Publishing, LLC
243 5th Avenue, Suite 136, New York, NY 10016

Copyright © 2019 by Cavendish Square Publishing, LLC

First Edition

Library of Congress Cataloging-in-Publication Data

Names: Boehme, Gerry author.
Title: How Hamilton made it to the stage / Gerry Boehme.
Description: New York : Cavendish Square, 2019. | Series: Getting to Broadway | Includes bibliographical references and index. | Audience: Grades 7-12.
Identifiers: LCCN 2017048054 (print) | LCCN 2017052222 (ebook) | ISBN 9781502635051 (library bound) | ISBN 9781502635075 (pbk.) | ISBN 9781502635068 (ebook)
Subjects: LCSH: Miranda, Lin-Manuel, 1980- Hamilton--Juvenile literature. | Hamilton, Alexander, 1757-1804--Drama--Juvenile literature.
Classification: LCC ML3930.M644 (ebook) | LCC ML3930.M644 B64 2018 (print) | DDC 792.6/42--dc23
LC record available at https://lccn.loc.gov/2017048054

Editorial Director: David McNamara
Editor: Fletcher Doyle/Tracey Maciejewski
Copy Editor: Rebecca Rohan
Associate Art Director: Amy Greenan
Designer: Lindsey Auten
Production Coordinator: Karol Szymczuk
Photo Research: J8 Media

The photographs in this book are used by permission and through the courtesy of: Cover, p. 4 Theo Wargo/WireImage/Getty Images; p. 11 Print Collector/Hulton Archive/Getty Images; p. 17 ©AP Images; p. 20 ©iStockphoto.com/Rocky89; p. 23 Gary Gershoff/WireImage/Getty Images; p. 29 Jenny Anderson/WireImage/Getty Images; pp. 41, 46 Walter McBride/Getty Images; p. 42 Brent N. Clarke/Getty Images; p. 66 White House Photo/Alamy Stock Photo.

Printed in the United States of America

Contents

Chapter 1

Making History Sing

I n July 2008, Lin-Manuel Miranda needed a vacation. A man of many talents, Miranda was a twenty-eight-year-old author, playwright, actor, singer, musician, and songwriter who had just reached the pinnacle of success when his Broadway show *In the Heights* won four Tony Awards. Looking to take a well-deserved break, Miranda and his wife-to-be booked a trip to Mexico.

Before he left, Miranda bought a copy of author Ron Chernow's exhaustive, 700-plus-page historical biography *Alexander Hamilton*, which described the life and accomplishments of one of the most important Founding Fathers of the United States. Miranda was just looking for something to read at the beach; little did he know that his

Opposite: Lin-Manuel Miranda's musical *Hamilton* tells the story of Alexander Hamilton, one of America's most important Founding Fathers.

random choice for a book would not only change his life, but the face of Broadway itself.

Book To Musical

Seven years later, on July 13, 2015, Lin-Manuel Miranda's new musical, *Hamilton*, held its first preview performance on Broadway at the Richard Rodgers Theatre in New York City. The street buzz for *Hamilton* had already reached a fever pitch; the show had just completed a short but wildly successful off-Broadway run at the Public Theater downtown. Audiences and critics alike raved about the show's unique and exciting blend of high-energy hip-hop music, performed by a racially diverse cast, mixed with detailed history lessons about the men and women who founded the United States.

As the audience settled into their seats, the actor playing the infamous Aaron Burr opened the play by chanting, in hip-hop rhythm, these opening lines:

> How does a bastard, orphan, son of a whore and a Scotsman, dropped in the middle of a forgotten spot in the Caribbean by Providence, impoverished, in squalor,
> Grow up to be a hero and a scholar?

That opening question dramatically introduced Alexander Hamilton's life story: how did an immigrant child from the Caribbean rise from poverty to become one of the key people involved in establishing the United States? It's a fascinating story.

The same kinds of questions can be asked about the musical *Hamilton* itself. How in the world did a play about a man who lived more than two hundred years ago take Broadway by storm?

Unlikely Success

Alexander Hamilton may be the least known of the Founding Fathers, far less celebrated than more familiar historical giants like George Washington and Thomas Jefferson. Hamilton never served as President of the United States; he was killed by fellow statesman Aaron Burr in a duel while only in his forties. How could he become the subject of one of the most popular Broadway musicals of all time?

Even more astonishing, *Hamilton* broke almost all the rules in the traditional Broadway musical playbook. It starred primarily African American and Hispanic actors and its music featured rapid-fire hip-hop lyrics and rap rhymes that echoed the diverse neighborhoods of inner cities.

In many ways, the story behind the musical *Hamilton* mirrors the life led by Alexander Hamilton himself. Rising from humble origins, Hamilton did not fit the typical image of a leader or follow the expected path. Yet he rose to become one of the most influential people in American history. *Hamilton* the musical followed an equally unlikely path on its way to achieving unexpected and unrivaled success on the Broadway stage.

The stories of Alexander Hamilton the man, and *Hamilton* the musical, are powerfully intertwined. By looking closely at one, the other comes into better view.

Who Was Alexander Hamilton?

For many people, Alexander Hamilton represents little more than the historical face that stares back at them from the US ten-dollar bill. Others more familiar with US history may recall that he died after being shot by Burr during a duel, or that he served in George Washington's army and as the first Secretary of the US Treasury. Perhaps they even recognize that Hamilton is the person most responsible for the creation of the nation's financial system.

Hamilton's full story, however, is a lot more complicated, and a lot more interesting, than that.

Hamilton was born on January 11 on the island of Nevis in the British West Indies. His exact year of birth remains unclear. Biographer Ron Chernow says it could be either 1755 or 1757, and he decided to use 1755 as the official date when he wrote his biography.

A Hard Childhood

Years before Hamilton's birth, his mother Rachel left her cruel husband and moved to the island of Saint Kitts. There, she met a Scottish trader named James Hamilton, and they had two sons, James Jr. (born in 1753) and Alexander, born after they moved to Nevis. James Hamilton eventually abandoned Rachel and the boys, leaving them poor and struggling.

Alexander Hamilton was smart and wanted to improve his life. He started working when he was only eleven and later took a job on the island of Saint Croix as an accounting clerk, where he learned about business and trade. Rachel Hamilton became ill and died in 1768 at the age of thirty-eight, but that only made Alexander work even harder. Hamilton impressed his boss and other businessmen so much that they pooled their money to send him to America for an education.

Hamilton was only about sixteen when he arrived in New York in 1773. He enrolled in King's College (now Columbia University) but found himself drawn to politics. Times were tense; the American colonies were moving toward open revolt against Great Britain over taxes and regulations the colonists thought to be unfair. Hamilton sided with the colonists and soon left college to support their cause.

Joining The Fight

Hamilton joined the Continental Army and fought in several battles, eventually being promoted to lieutenant colonel. He caught the eye of General George Washington, who took him on as an assistant and advisor. Hamilton turned out to be an excellent and persuasive writer; he composed many of Washington's letters as well as reports on the war and how to organize the army. He also married Elizabeth Schuyler, whose wealthy family lived in New York.

After a time, Hamilton grew frustrated with not being closer to the war. He managed to convince Washington to let him return to the battlefield, and he later helped lead a winning charge against the British in the Battle of Yorktown in 1781.

Hamilton continued to serve George Washington as he built the first United States government after the victory over the British. It wouldn't be an easy job. While the colonies had united to rid themselves of British rule, they now argued about whether states should control their own affairs and finances or grant more power to the new central government.

The Case for Federal Control

Hamilton strongly believed that creating a strong central, or federal, government would be the key to building a lasting American nation. He argued that the central government needed money to be financially strong, and he proposed that the federal government collect taxes from the states while assuming all their debts from the war.

Hamilton's passionate support for a strong federal government put him at odds with some of the other leaders who helped America become independent. People like Thomas Jefferson and James Madison feared putting too much power in the hands of a central government and wanted to leave many responsibilities in the hands of the former colonies.

When George Washington was elected the first president of the United States in 1789, he appointed Hamilton as the first Secretary of the United States Treasury. One of the Hamilton's accomplishments was to work out a secret deal with James Madison of Virginia to move the nation's capital south from New York to a location near Virginia (now Washington, DC) in return for Virginia's support for stronger central government. The back-room

Alexander Hamilton was born on Nevis, an island in the British West Indies.

aspects of the discussions came to be known as the "dinner table bargain" and provided the basis for a powerful song in *Hamilton* ("The Room Where It Happens").

For a time, Hamilton left political life to establish his law practice in New York City. During those years, he won cases that established important legal principles such as the right of due process and the way that higher courts review lower court decisions. He also helped found the Bank of New York. However, Hamilton remained active in politics for the rest of his life.

From Friend to Enemy

While Hamilton's childhood was difficult, Aaron Burr was born to a wealthy New Jersey family in 1756. Like Hamilton, Burr was very intelligent and served in the Continental Army. He also was very interested in politics.

As the musical shows, Alexander Hamilton and Aaron Burr started out as friends and allies. As years passed, however, the two men grew to intensely dislike one another. Burr thought Hamilton was too aggressive, while Hamilton felt that Burr wanted power at any price and would never take a clear position. It didn't help that Burr ran against and beat Hamilton's father-in-law for a seat in the New York Senate in 1790. When Burr ran for Vice President of the United States in 1796, Hamilton helped defeat him. Burr ran again in the next national election and tied Thomas Jefferson in presidential votes, but Hamilton once again used his influence and helped elect Jefferson. Hamilton later opposed Burr's campaign for Governor of New York in 1804.

That was the last straw for Burr, especially since he considered Hamilton's attacks to be personal as well as political. He challenged Hamilton to a duel and, on July 11, 1804 in Weehawken, New Jersey, Burr shot Hamilton.

Hamilton died the next day in New York. Hamilton's wife Eliza lived for fifty more years and dedicated her life to preserving Hamilton's legacy.

On a Whim

While it may sound like a tale that's too good to be true, Lin-Manuel Miranda really did buy Ron Chernow's book *Alexander Hamilton* by chance while heading for a vacation in Mexico. Miranda later told the story to interviewer Charlie Rose during an episode of the CBS television program *60 Minutes*, recalling that, "I was just browsing the biography section. It could have been [former President] Truman."

Miranda admits that he didn't know much about Alexander Hamilton before he read Chernow's book. He told *Atlantic* magazine:

> I wrote a paper on Hamilton in high school. And it was just about the duel. That's what most people focus on. And that's really all I knew when I grabbed Ron's book off the shelf. The sort of thinking that went into it was, "This will have a good ending." Ron's book was a really acclaimed, well-reviewed book and biography, and I was just looking for a good biography to read on the beach.

As Miranda read through Chernow's biography, he felt an emotional connection to Hamilton's life story. Hamilton was an immigrant; Miranda's own parents had immigrated to the United States from Puerto Rico. He also shared Chernow's view that Hamilton has been overlooked and misunderstood compared to other Founding Fathers like George Washington and Thomas Jefferson.

Lots of Research

Miranda realized from the very beginning that he was embarking on a very complicated project that would be viewed, and judged, by people from many different backgrounds. Miranda's *Hamilton* depicts the life of Alexander Hamilton during a crucial time of American history, including the Revolutionary period as well as the formation of the US government after the colonies won their independence from Great Britain. From a practical standpoint, Alexander Hamilton himself was a complex and controversial figure.

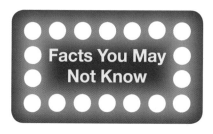

EXTRA WORK

Miranda wrote parts of *Hamilton* while playing the role of a doctor in the 2013 television series *Do No Harm*. The show was filmed in Philadelphia, which Miranda found to be a perfect place to research Alexander Hamilton.

Ron Chernow took more than seven hundred pages to tell Alexander Hamilton's story, but Miranda's Broadway musical had to tell that same story in less than three hours. Miranda knew he needed to get it right; Miranda repeatedly stated that he wanted to keep his play as close to history as he could. "I felt an enormous responsibility to be as historically accurate as possible, while still telling the most dramatic story possible," Miranda told the *Atlantic* in a 2015 interview.

One of Miranda's first steps was to recruit Chernow as an advisor. Miranda also knew, however, that he might have to veer a bit from a strict historical path when creative elements of the show demanded it. He said:

> When I did part from the historical record or take dramatic license, I made sure I was able to defend it to Ron, because I knew that I was going to have to defend it in the real world. None of those choices are made lightly.

Delving Deeper

While Chernow's biography certainly gave Miranda a great start, he knew that the book would be just his first building block. Miranda searched out Hamilton's original letters and works. He intended to make Aaron Burr a main character in his show, so he read another biography, *The Heartbreak of Aaron Burr* by H.W. Brands, so he could gain a better understanding of the man who shifted from being a close friend of Hamilton to a rival, and eventually his killer. Alexander Hamilton and

THE BOOK THAT STARTED IT ALL

Ron Chernow wrote the biography that inspired Lin-Manuel Miranda to conceive the Broadway musical *Hamilton*.

Born in 1949, Chernow graduated with honors from both Yale in the United States (undergraduate degree) and Cambridge University (graduate degree) in the United Kingdom. Chernow has also worked as a journalist and a business executive, but he is best known for his biographies about famous people.

In April 2004, Chernow published *Alexander Hamilton* to rave reviews. The *New York Times* praised it as "moving and masterly ... by far the best biography ever written about the man." Many praised Chernow for bringing Hamilton's character to life in ways no one had done before. Some reviewer comments echo Lin-Manuel Miranda's own reaction when he read the book.

TimeOut New York's John Freeman wrote that "Alexander Hamilton has been overshadowed by the Founding Fathers he served under ... Ron Chernow's magisterial biography will certainly change that." *Newsweek's* David Gates said that the book justified Chernow's claim that "Hamilton's life was the most dramatic and improbable life among the Founding Fathers" and that Chernow "shows all Hamilton's complexity." Steve Raymond's review in the *Seattle Times* noted that Hamilton's life was "so tumultuous that only an audacious novelist could have dreamed it up." Larry Cox wrote in the *Tucson Citizen* that

"Chernow sorts out this period in history and humanizes Hamilton."

During an interview on *60 Minutes*, Chernow described what it was about Hamilton's life that inspired him to write his biography. "He creates the first fiscal system, first monetary system, first customs service, first central bank, on, and on, and on," he said. "Here's the story of a penniless, orphaned, immigrant kid who comes out of nowhere and sets the world on fire. He was born on the island of Nevis. He spent his adolescence in Saint Croix. His

Ron Chernow, author of the biography *Alexander Hamilton* that inspired Lin-Manuel Miranda's musical

father abandoned the family when Alexander was eleven. His mother died when he was thirteen. When he came to North America, he didn't know a soul. And his achievements were absolutely monumental."

Chernow's *Alexander Hamilton* spent three months on the New York Times bestseller list and was the first recipient of the George Washington Book Prize for the year's best book about the founding era. After the *Hamilton* musical made its smash debut on Broadway, the biography returned to the bestseller lists and sold another million copies. The book has been translated into fifteen languages.

Chernow achieved more success when he released his biography of George Washington, *Washington: A Life*, in October 2010 and won the Pulitzer Prize. In September 2017, President Barack Obama awarded him a National Humanities Medal at the White House.

his son were both killed in duels, so Miranda read *Affairs of Honor* by Joanne Freeman so he could get more background on how duels were arranged and conducted.

Miranda also read Chernow's biography of George Washington to gain more insight into Washington's character and how he might interact with Alexander Hamilton in the play.

Following History

Lin-Manuel Miranda did indeed get the history right, especially considering that musicals are meant to entertain and inspire as well as inform. Most of *Hamilton*'s scenes and songs are based on actual events, and Miranda's lyrics often quote the words and writings of Hamilton and other characters. One song contains language from George Washington's farewell address. In "Right Hand Man," Washington sings, "Are these the men with which I am to defend America?" Washington once said those exact words when talking about his soldiers in a rare fit of temper.

Miranda also portrays some *Hamilton* scenes in his own way while trying to preserve the spirit of the actual historical event. For example, the song "The Reynolds Pamphlet" dramatizes a long letter that Hamilton wrote to explain a romantic affair that he had with a woman named Maria Reynolds that almost ruined his marriage. The pamphlet was real, but Miranda updated some of Hamilton's original language to make it sound more contemporary. In another case, Miranda used actual lyrics from an English soldiers' drinking song of the time ("The World Turned Upside Down"), but he wrote a new melody.

Miranda fully admits, however, that in some cases he changed scenes, or even made them up, in order to better portray the drama behind Alexander Hamilton's story. While some criticize Miranda's failure to strictly adhere to every historical fact, others believe that Miranda did a great job of telling history in an entertaining, dramatic way and making Hamilton's story come alive to today's audiences.

Ron Chernow's biography and Lin-Manuel Miranda's musical both portray Hamilton's long path from young dreamer to unlikely Founding Father. Miranda's *Hamilton* followed a similar journey. Born as a dream in the mind of a son of immigrants, *Hamilton* went on to navigate and conquer the challenging path to Broadway, driven by Miranda's talent and determination as well as invaluable support from his partners.

RODGERS
HAMILTON
AN AMERICAN MUSICAL
HAMILTON
AN AMERICAN MUSICAL
RODGERS
HAMILTON
RICHARD
RODGERS
2C93
1D82
6P44

From Mixtape to the Stage

The Richard Rodgers Theatre opened in 1924 as the 46th Street Theatre, named for the street where it stood in the heart of New York City's Broadway district. It was renamed in 1990 in honor of legendary composer Richard Rodgers, whose shows brightened Broadway for many years.

The Richard Rodgers Theatre has hosted many great musicals over its history, but none garnered more attention than its current resident, *Hamilton* (as of 2017). Audiences have packed its 1,319 seats each night, eagerly waiting for the show to begin. Most people have waited more than a year, and paid hundreds or perhaps even thousands of dollars, to be present for that moment.

Opposite: Hamilton drew rave reviews and sold-out performances when it opened at the Richard Rodgers Theatre on Broadway.

Hamilton's Own Story

What awaits is an award-winning blockbuster that people will likely talk about for months afterward. Others may listen to the original Broadway cast's audio recording or the *Hamilton Mixtape*, a collection of remixes, covers, and songs inspired by the originals, or see *Hamilton* performed in another city, and experience something very similar—an awe-inspiring mix of artistic creativity and energetic performance that continues to expand the legion of *Hamilton* fans.

Roll back the curtain and another, equally compelling story emerges. You think Alexander Hamilton lived an interesting life? The musical *Hamilton* boasts an intriguing backstory as well. Years of development, total shifts in approach and emphasis, spirited discussions among creative and financial partners—*Hamilton* came to life only after traveling down a long, twisting path that began more than six years before its opening night on Broadway.

Reaching the Heights

When Lin-Manuel Miranda wrote the music and lyrics for his Tony Award-winning musical *In the Heights*, he mixed the sounds of salsa music with the rap rhymes and hip-hop rhythms from his own New York City Washington Heights neighborhood, where the show takes place. For many audience members, *In the Heights* represented their first real exposure to rap and hip-hop.

Rap describes a musical style in which words are spoken with an emphasis on their rhythm and rhyme.

Lin-Manuel Miranda also featured rap and hip-hop in his previous Broadway musical *In the Heights*.

While hip-hop describes the backing music for rap speech, in reality, it's much more than that. Hip-hop defines a culture with many different elements, including rap speech, deejaying (or turntabling), dance, style and attitude. Hip-hop originated in the predominantly African American South Bronx of New York City in the late 1970s.

Portraying hip-hop culture on the Broadway stage was certainly unusual. For Miranda, however, hip-hop helped him tell his story about Washington Heights by including the same language, music, and movements that his characters would likely use in their daily life.

Hip-Hop Hamilton?

After reading Chernow's biography of Hamilton, Lin-Manuel Miranda was, in his words, "thunderstruck." At first glance, Hamilton's eighteenth-century world doesn't seem to have much in common with present-day Washington Heights. In his creative mind, however, Miranda began to picture this dynamic historical figure in the same way he viewed contemporary rap and hip-hop artists he admired.

> I got to the part where a hurricane destroys St. Croix, where Hamilton is living. And he writes a poem about the carnage and this poem gets him off the island … I drew a direct line between Hamilton's writing his way out of his circumstances and the rappers I'd grown up adoring. It's Biggie and Jay-Z writing about growing up in the Marcy Projects in Brooklyn. It's Eminem writing about growing up white in Detroit. It's writing about that struggle and paradoxically your writing being so good it gets you out.

Miranda told the *New York Times* that Hamilton's story is "part and parcel with the hip-hop narrative: writing your way out of your circumstances, writing the future you want to see for yourself."

Right from the beginning, Lin-Manuel realized he faced a major challenge. Chernow's book was long, but Broadway musicals typically run well under three hours, including intermission. Even more challenging, musicals contain much less spoken dialogue than dramas; they bring their characters' thoughts and emotions to life through their songs. Miranda needed to "sing" Hamilton's complex history, and he needed to pack an awful lot of information into each song.

Originally Just Music

Miranda told the *New York Times* that "I wanted the lyrics to have the density that my favorite hip-hop albums have … It was easier to think of it as a hip-hop album, because then I could really just pack the lyrics."

When he first imagined telling Hamilton's story through hip-hop, Miranda didn't think of it as a Broadway musical. In fact, his idea was to produce a mixtape, a collection of hip-hop songs by different artists that he would record. As he started talking to others about his idea, he began referring to it as "The Hamilton Mixtape."

"I always had an eye toward the stage for the story of Hamilton's life, but I began with the idea of a concept album, the way Andrew Lloyd Webber's *Evita* and *Jesus Christ Superstar* were albums before they were musicals," Miranda told the *Hollywood Reporter*. Miranda even imagined some of his favorite hip-hop artists like Common, Busta Rhymes, and Eminem in leading roles.

Crucial Support

The idea of using hip-hop to tell Hamilton's story made sense to him, but Miranda wasn't sure if anyone else would agree. Luckily, at that earliest stage, he received critical and immediate support from one of the people closest to him—Vanessa Nadal, the woman who would soon become his wife.

In his book *Hamilton: The Revolution*, Miranda wrote, "When I looked up from that Chernow book and said, 'I think this is a hip-hop musical,' she [Vanessa] didn't laugh, or roll her eyes. She just said, 'That sounds cool.' And that was all I needed to get started."

Nadal knew that Miranda had trouble writing when he was home in New York; he was always being interrupted and pulled in different directions by his many contacts and project ideas. So, Miranda said, Nadal "booked us trips and time away from New York … Thanks to her, *Hamilton* was written in Mexico, Spain, Nevis, Sagaponack [eastern Long Island], St. Croix, Puerto Rico, and the Dominican Republic—long trips where Vanessa would take me there and then leave me alone to write while she explored."

Miranda was now ready to get serious about his "Hamilton Mixtape" project. He knew he would need a lot of help, and he had no doubt about where he should start.

Get Chernow

Soon after he returned from the vacation in Mexico that stoked his imagination, Miranda decided to reach out to the person who helped start it all—author Ron Chernow. He managed to get Chernow's email address, and he invited the famous author to attend his musical *In the Heights*. Right after the show ended, Miranda told Chernow about his Hamilton project and asked him to be his historical consultant. Miranda told him, "I want historians to take this seriously."

Chernow may have had some doubts at first. His book, *Alexander Hamilton*, had attracted widespread attention since it was published in 2004, but Chernow had also experienced a bit of disappointment. Hollywood studios had optioned his biography three times, but they had never followed through in making a movie. Chernow wasn't sure at first if Miranda meant what he said, but he quickly learned how serious Miranda was.

As an important first step, Miranda followed through and optioned Chernow's book. The author was happy that *Alexander Hamilton* would finally get more attention, but he never thought that attention would come via a hip-hop musical. As time passed and Miranda worked on other projects, he continued to check in with Chernow to ask questions about Hamilton and other characters, including what they may have been thinking at certain times and what small details Miranda could add to scenes to make them more realistic.

Chernow proved to be a willing and valuable teammate. Chernow told the *New York Times Magazine* that Miranda's *Hamilton* is "pretty close to who historians know the Founding Father to be … I think [Miranda] has plucked out the dramatic essence of the character—his vaulting ambition, his obsession with his legacy, his driven nature, his roving eye, his brilliant mind, his faulty judgment."

Seeing The Vision

Recruiting Chernow represented an important step for Miranda. Other early supporters played a key role as

THE GENIUS BEHIND *HAMILTON*

Lin-Manuel Miranda was born on January 16, 1980 in New York City and grew up with his older sister Luz in northern Manhattan. His parents emigrated from Puerto Rico; his father, Luis Miranda, works as a political consultant and his mother, Luz Towns-Miranda, is a psychologist.

Music filled Miranda's childhood home, and he grew up listening to a wide range of musical styles, ranging from salsa records to the cast albums from famous Broadway plays. He attended his first Broadway show (*Les Misérables*) when he was seven and caught the Broadway musical bug. His mother recalls that her son "loved to sing. He was always creating, and he loved words and songs."

At five, Miranda entered a school for highly gifted children, where he sometimes felt he didn't belong. "I was surrounded by genius kids," Miranda says now, so he knew he had to "figure out what it is I wanna do and work really hard at that … [So] I picked a lane, and I started running."

Miranda chose the theater as his lane. He starred in school plays, winning the lead role of the Pirate King in *The Pirates of Penzance* as a high school freshman. He knew even then that he had found his calling in life. "All the girls have to pretend to fall in love with you, and all the guys have to pretend to follow you," he said. "Why would I do anything else for a living?"

He first imagined telling his own stories when he was seventeen and saw *Rent* on Broadway. *Rent* told the story of people living in a present-day New York neighborhood, using the familiar music and lyrics taken from those same streets. "The notion that a musical could take place today and sound like today was groundbreaking to me," he remembers.

Lin-Manuel Miranda wrote the story, music, and lyrics for *Hamilton* and also played the lead role.

Miranda imagined merging traditional Broadway with the Latin and hip-hop music he also adored. While attending Wesleyan University, he conceived and wrote *In the Heights*. After graduating, Miranda partnered with fellow Wesleyan graduate and aspiring director Thomas (Tommy) Kail to bring *In the Heights* to Broadway, where it won four Tony Awards in 2008, including one for best musical.

"It was the beginning of a conversation that's never stopped," says Kail. That conversation goes on today as *Hamilton* continues to sell out in New York, Chicago, and other cities around the country.

well. Jeremy McCarter was the drama critic at *New York* magazine when Miranda's first show, *In the Heights*, premiered off-Broadway in 2007. McCarter had already written articles in favor of using hip-hop in musicals; he actually began one of his essays by writing "Hip-hop can save the theater."

McCarter thought that Broadway musicals had become stale and that hip-hop could help. He remembers thinking that "Rap … wasn't like rock or jazz or any other kind of pop music. The lyrical density and storytelling ingenuity I heard … seemed closer to the verbal energy of the great plays of the past than almost anything I saw onstage." Few of McCarter's colleagues at the time agreed with him, however.

When McCarter first saw *In the Heights*, he thought he had found a kindred spirit. *Heights* "made me sit up in my aisle seat: Here's the guy," McCarter wrote later. "Lin's show about immigrants in Upper Manhattan fused salsa, hip-hop, and traditional Broadway ballads to make something old and new, familiar and surprising. Best of all, he made the leap that virtually nobody else had made, using hip-hop to tell a story that had nothing to do with hip-hop—using it as form, not content."

McCarter and Miranda soon met and quickly became friends, and Miranda told McCarter of his vision to create "The Hamilton Mixtape." Neither man realized at the time that those first conversations would lead to several more years of brainstorming and sharing ideas as Miranda worked on different pieces of his mixtape while he also pursued other projects.

White House Rap

Miranda now had some support for his mixtape idea, but he had no way of knowing how people outside of his inner circle might react to his revolutionary approach. He found out in a big way on May 12, 2009.

Just a few weeks earlier, he had received a call from the White House. President Barack Obama and First Lady Michelle Obama were planning to host an evening of live performances including poetry and music, all intended to reflect "the American experience." Miranda was invited to participate and perform a song from *In the Heights*. He accepted the invitation, but he decided to take a huge risk.

It was only nine months after his vacation in Mexico, and he had just started working on his Hamilton project. When his turn came to appear at the White House, Miranda chose not to perform a selection from *In the Heights*, as expected. Instead, he surprised everyone that night by debuting the first song he had written for his mixtape. Standing in front of an audience that included the President, his wife, and their daughters, Miranda introduced the song by saying:

> I'm actually working on a hip-hop album. It's a concept album about the life of someone who I think embodies hip-hop, Treasury Secretary Alexander Hamilton. You laugh?! But it's true!

Miranda then revealed another surprise—that he'd sing the song from the perspective of another famous historical figure, Hamilton's one-time friend and eventual killer, Aaron

Burr. Accompanied only by his friend Alex Lacamoire on piano, Miranda invited his audience to snap their fingers to the rhythm as he launched into what became the opening song for *Hamilton*.

WOW!

To say that Miranda won over the White House audience that night would be a tremendous understatement. The audience, including the first family, broke into broad smiles as soon as Miranda spun out his first rap rhyme. When he finished, the crowd jumped to their feet, showering Miranda and Lacamoire with a standing ovation.

For Lin-Manuel Miranda, the audience's enthusiastic reception validated his own passion for the project. "I say, 'Hip-hop, Alexander Hamilton,' and everyone laughs. And then, by the end, they're not laughing. Because they're in it. Because they've been sucked into the story, just like I got sucked into the story."

Hamilton was on its way! But, getting it onto the Broadway stage would still prove to be a long and winding road.

Hit The Pause Button

Miranda continued to work on his "Hamilton Mixtape" for the next two years, but he took on many other projects as well. Miranda helped write the score for a musical named *Bring It On*, and he translated some lyrics from *West Side Story* into Spanish for a Broadway revival. He also wrote the closing rap number for host Neil Patrick Harris at the 2011 Tony Awards, he celebrated his thirtieth and thirty-first birthdays, and he performed with his improv hip-hop group Freestyle Love Supreme.

Then, in June 2011, Miranda was invited to perform at a benefit concert. He decided it was time to premiere the second song, "My Shot" from his mixtape. Miranda's close friend, Tommy Kail, happened to be sitting in the audience. Miranda had already talked a bit with Kail about his idea.

Miranda and Kail both graduated from Wesleyan University in Connecticut, where Miranda had written *In the Heights*. They later partnered to bring *Heights* to Broadway, with Kail as director. After college, Miranda and Kail also worked together putting on hip-hop improv shows with Freestyle Love Supreme, along with future *Hamilton* castmates Christopher Jackson and Daveed Diggs (a rapper from the West Coast), and occasional help from Alex Lacamoire.

When Miranda performed "My Shot," the crowd loved it. Hearing the reaction, Kail knew that the time was now; people really wanted to hear more about Hamilton's story. He met with Miranda after the show and pleaded with his friend to get serious about developing the Hamilton project. Kail suggested that Miranda send him material on a regular basis and proposed that they plan a concert of Hamilton songs in six months.

Fate?

The stakes rose quickly. Just a few days later, New York's famous complex for the performing arts, Lincoln Center, invited Miranda to perform for its American Songbook concert series. Kail thought it could be an excellent way to try out some mixtape songs, even though it put a lot pressure on Miranda to put enough material together. Still, how they could pass up this chance?

It seemed like destiny was on their side. Lincoln Center's proposed date—January 11— happened to fall on Alexander Hamilton's birthday.

It's A Musical!

Miranda and Kail expected their show in the Allen Room at Lincoln Center to be informal and fun, and they invited several of their friends to perform. When the show started, however, they were surprised to see that all 450 seats were filled; many heavyweights from the media and New York theater had come to hear this new idea from the composer of *In the Heights*. After Miranda and his friends performed twelve songs, two things became clear: 1) The audience loved what they had done; 2) Many weren't quite sure how to describe what they had just seen and heard.

Perhaps Stephen Holden said it best in his review for the *New York Times*:

> **Is The Hamilton Mixtape ... a future Broadway musical? A concept album? A multimedia extravaganza in search of a platform? Does it even matter? What it is, is hot.**

To Broadway producer Jeffrey Seller, the answer was obvious. "It became crystal clear ... that it was a Broadway show," he remembers. Lin had played some songs for him the night before, but seeing them performed in front of an audience led Sellers to think, "Here's the show. The musical has emerged. This makes dramatic sense ... Even in a concert format, the story was taking shape."

Just a few weeks later, the next phase of *Hamilton*'s story unfolded.

Opportunity Knocks

Miranda's friend Jeremy McCarter had left the magazine business and joined the artistic staff of New York's Public Theater, an arts organization known for showcasing exciting new playwrights and performers. In the summer of 2011, the theater's artistic director, Oskar Eustis, asked McCarter to recommend some artists and projects for their next season.

"The first artist who came to mind was Lin," McCarter wrote when recalling what happened next, "and the first project was his Hamilton idea."

McCarter arranged for Miranda and Eustis to meet. After that, Miranda sent audio demos to Eustis, while Eustis attended some of Miranda's concerts.

No Talking

Meanwhile, the *Hamilton* team made a critically important decision. When Miranda and his collaborators decided to make *Hamilton* a musical, they assumed that the show would include dialogue as well as songs. Traditional musicals often use spoken lines to connect the songs and scenes. Adding dialogue for *Hamilton* would require an experienced playwright.

At first, that was good news for Miranda. Up until then, he was writing everything in the show; adding a team member to write dialogue would certainly lessen the load that Miranda was carrying at the time. The plan, however, didn't work. The team asked a playwright they respected to write some scenes, but a single reading convinced everyone that spoken words could not possibly sustain the energy that Miranda's rapped lyrics already provided.

All of the responsibility now fell on Lin-Manuel Miranda's shoulders; he would have to write everything, and his song lyrics would have to tell Alexander Hamilton's entire story.

Heading Upstate

In July 2013, the *Hamilton* team received an invitation to take part in the New York Stage and Film series of developmental workshops at Vassar College, located near Poughkeepsie, NY. On a hot Saturday afternoon, 150 people packed Vassar's Powerhouse Theater to see what *Hamilton* had become.

Accompanied only by Alex Lacamoire on piano and Scott Wasserman using musical-production software, and with no scenery or staging, Miranda and his troupe performed what turned out to be something very close to the final version of Act One, as well as a couple of songs from Act Two. It included everything Miranda had written up to that point.

Young performer Leslie Odom Jr. happened to be seated in the last row; he had come to see his wife appear in another workshop. Odom was amazed when Miranda and his friends performed their *Hamilton* songs. Afterward, Odom sent Miranda a text raving about the show, telling him that he would be *Hamilton*'s biggest cheerleader when it opened. Instead, Miranda and Kail recruited him to join the *Hamilton* cast, offering him the chance to play Aaron Burr.

Dream Team

The *Hamilton* team was coming into focus; many of them had already worked together. Lacamoire was on board to handle music, and Kail signed on as director. Choreographer Andy Blankenbuehler had already won a Tony and other awards for his work on *In the Heights*. Paul Tazewell had twenty years of experience designing costumes for Broadway shows; he was also a *Heights* veteran.

The performing cast took shape as well. Miranda would continue to play Alexander Hamilton, and Leslie Odom Jr. had joined as Aaron Burr. Christopher Jackson (as George Washington) and Daveed Diggs (playing both Marquis de Lafayette and Thomas Jefferson) were also set. But, there were still some important roles to fill.

Most of *Hamilton*'s scenes take place in eighteenth-century New York City; one of the show's early songs calls New York "the greatest city in the world." To set the mood, Miranda and his team needed a set designer who could link the scenes on stage to the real-life, vibrant streets that lived just outside the theater doors. Tommy Kail found the perfect partner in David Korins.

Korins had already worked with the *Hamilton* creative team and experienced his own success on Broadway. Nonetheless, Korins still worked hard to prepare for his interview with Kail. He listened to Miranda's demos and sketched out stage ideas, building a strong connection to the show. "We all have something to prove here," Korins told Kail and, paraphrasing a line from one of the big musical numbers, "I am not going to throw away my shot." He got the job.

HAMILTON? OR BURR?
Lin-Manuel Miranda had trouble deciding whether to play Alexander Hamilton or Aaron Burr. "I feel an equal affinity with Burr," Miranda said. "[He] is every bit as smart as Hamilton ... and he comes from the same amount of loss."

Picking a Producer

Miranda now had the creative elements covered, but he still needed someone to put it all together. Musicals are complicated projects with many moving parts to manage; they also require a lot of financial support. *Hamilton* needed a producer.

Jeffrey Seller and his partner Kevin McCollum had produced eight Broadway shows together, including *Rent* and *Avenue Q*. Most of them, Seller later recalled, were about "young people asking themselves: Who am I? What am I going to do with my life? What is my purpose?"

It was McCollum who first met Lin-Manuel Miranda at an early reading of *In the Heights* in 2004. Seller and McCollum later joined with Jill Furman to produce *In the Heights* on Broadway.

A few weeks after Seller saw the *Hamilton* performance at Lincoln Center, he took Miranda to lunch and told him, "If you want me to produce your show, I'd love to produce your show." Shortly after that, Seller sent an email to Miranda and Kail, offering to be a "passionate advocate, cheerleader, sounding board, constructive critic, and barker."

Seller seemed like the right choice, but there was one big issue. Seller and McCollum had ended their partnership in 2012 and no longer worked together. Miranda and Kail knew and respected both men, which made the decision on choosing a producer for *Hamilton* a difficult one. "It was a situation we didn't ask to be in," Miranda later said. In the end, they decided to partner with Seller.

Public Exposure

On July 30, 2013, three days after the Vassar performance, Miranda and Kail met Seller for lunch in Manhattan to talk about what would come next for *Hamilton*. Miranda and Kail wanted to mount a full production by the end of 2014, even though they still didn't have a complete second act. They also agreed that any hip-hop musical about a Founding Father who lived in New York City simply *had* to premiere in New York!

After visiting several off-Broadway theaters they thought might be a good fit for *Hamilton*, Seller summarized their unanimous decision.

"I want to go to the Public."

THE BUSINESS OF BROADWAY

Born in 1965, *Hamilton* Producer Jeffrey Seller graduated from the University of Michigan before moving to New York City to work in the business side of theater. Teaming with partner Kevin McCollum, Seller produced many Broadway shows, including three that won the Tony Award for Best Musical: *Rent* (1996), *Avenue Q* (2003), and *In the Heights* (2008).

So, what exactly does a Broadway producer do, anyway?

While Broadway shows celebrate art and creativity, the harsh reality is that they also exist as businesses and need to make money. Investors provide large sums of cash in the hope that, if a show is successful, they will receive far-greater profits. If the show flops, they lose everything.

Off-Broadway musicals might cost around $2 million to bring to the stage, and a Broadway drama might cost $3 million to $6 million. Broadway musicals, however, cost a lot more; expenses include orchestras, bigger casts, scenery, and sometimes even lavish special effects. The average Broadway musical requires $8 million to $12 million in up-front investment just to make it to opening night. Some musicals cost far more; it is reported that the 2010 disaster *Spiderman: Turn Off The Dark* cost, and quickly lost, more than $75 million!

Successful musicals, on the other hand, can make millions of dollars for their creators. Profits from *Hamilton* are divided among Lin-Manuel Miranda and his team, including the producers and Ron Chernow, as well as approximately one hundred investors. Less than a year after *Hamilton* opened, in March 2016, it was reported that investors had already made all their money back.

Producer Jeffrey Seller worked with the *Hamilton* cast to bring the musical to Broadway.

More than anyone else, the Broadway producer walks the fine line between art and finance. Producers themselves describe their jobs in many different ways, ranging from "[We provide] the three F's: Find It (the show), Fund It, Fill The Seats" to "Make the best art possible with the available financial resources." No matter how they define their role, the need to balance creativity with profit always weighs heavily on a producer's mind.

After splitting up with former partner McCollum in 2012, Seller teamed once again with Miranda to produce *Hamilton*, saying that "We want people who come to New York to say: I want to see the Statue of Liberty, go to the top of the Empire State Building, walk in Central Park. And I want to see *Hamilton*."

Hamilton turned out to be a winning bet for everyone—artists, investors and audiences alike.

Chapter 3

Like Nothing You've Ever Seen

In March 2014, the Public Theater announced that Lin-Manuel Miranda, the famous composer of *In the Heights*, would stage his newest work as part of its 2014–2015 season. Formerly known as "The Hamilton Mixtape," Miranda's show had grown into what was now a full-fledged musical with a new name: *Hamilton*.

Hamilton's stay at the Public would be brief; performances were scheduled to begin on January 20, 2015, and end just a few weeks later, on February 22. As word of mouth spread, and the cast began performing a series of workshops to help the *Hamilton* team refine and develop the show, it was announced that the show would remain at the Public until May before beginning previews on Broadway in July.

Opposite: Hamilton's cast, costumes, and set design all contributed to its rousing success.

All On Board

Jeffrey Seller and two partners—Sander Jacobs and Jill Furman—would produce *Hamilton* and provide its financing. They got down to business by assembling a full cast and technical team to stage the new stage musical.

Thomas Kail stayed on as director. Lin-Manuel Miranda continued to perform the title role as he also worked to complete the music score and lyrics. Christopher Jackson (George Washington) and Daveed Diggs (Lafayette/Jefferson) also remained in the cast.

Jackson had known Miranda longer than any other major cast member and had previously starred in *In the Heights*. Bay Area rapper Daveed Diggs had never seen a Broadway show before he joined *Hamilton*. "I knew *Fiddler on the Roof*, because my mom really liked that and we always had the album around the house growing up, and that was about it," Diggs says. "But I was totally intrigued the second I heard the demos of the songs in *Hamilton* and read through the music. The rapping is good—that's what really got me."

Leslie Odom Jr. had already signed up to play Aaron Burr after seeing the workshop at Vassar. To strengthen the cast, the team added two key female players: Renée Elise Goldsberry to play Angelica Schuyler and Phillipa Soo to play Eliza Schuyler Hamilton.

Impressive Women

Renée Elise Goldsberry stunned Miranda, Kail, and Oskar Eustis, the artistic director of the Public Theater, when she auditioned for the role of Angelica. She faultlessly sang the rapid-fire lyrics of *Hamilton*'s "Satisfied" after seeing it for the first time only the previous night. "She's—so—fast," said Miranda, eyes wide. "It's from doing all that Shakespeare," Eustis explained.

Renée had indeed performed Shakespeare as part of the Public's *Shakespeare in the Park* programs. She had also performed in four Broadway shows and many times on television, and she sang in a Top 40 cover band. Renée and her husband had just adopted a child, and she was determined to stay at home for a while, but when her agents sent her a demo of "Satisfied," she decided she needed to be a part of *Hamilton*.

Kail had first seen Soo late in 2012 when she made her debut in an off-Broadway show after graduating from Juilliard, the prestigious school for the performing arts. "That girl … she's a star," Kail told Miranda the next day. "There's just something there." Kail invited her to read for the role of Eliza and, Miranda said later, "She was it from then on."

Sellout!

The "Hamilton Mixtape" performances had already generated a great deal of anticipation. When the Public Theater announced the limited run for *Hamilton*, tickets for all performances sold out well before the first show. Demand ran so high that the Public extended *Hamilton*'s run three times through May 3, 2015. Even then, ticket sales could not

Renée Elise Goldsberry (*center*), Jasmine Cephas Jones (*left*) and Phillipa Soo (*right*) play three strong women in *Hamilton*.

keep pace with the heavy demand, and seats were snapped up as soon as they became available.

When *Hamilton* finally premiered at the Public, the reviews were extraordinary. *Vogue*'s Adam Green wrote:

> With a stunning multiethnic cast under the masterly direction of Thomas Kail, [*Hamilton*] exploded onto the stage of the Public Theater in February for a three-month run, driving critics (including this one) mad with joy, drawing insanely starry crowds, sweeping the Obie, Lortel, and Drama Desk awards, and setting off a frenzy for tickets.

Public Theater artistic director Oskar Eustis said :

> Lin-Manuel Miranda is a marvel, but nothing could have prepared us for the astonishing achievement of *Hamilton*. Alexander Hamilton was born in the West Indies, the only Founding Father who was an immigrant, and Lin's genius is to tell the story of the birth of the United States as an immigrant's story. The energy, the passion, joy, tragedy, and raw intelligence of this show are stunning.

Ready Yet?

Hamilton's off-Broadway run had always been designed to accomplish two goals. First, test the public reaction to this new, full-length, hip-hop Broadway musical. Second, allow Miranda and the rest of the creative team to improve the show and work out any rough spots to get it ready for prime-time Broadway.

Hamilton's smashing success at the Public, along with its many awards, answered the first question loud and clear: people wanted to see it, and right now! That led the team to consider whether *Hamilton* should move to Broadway sooner than planned. That discussion turned out to generate some drama of its own.

Demand and Supply

The Public is not really a theater; it's actually a complex that includes five different theaters located at its downtown New York City location. *Hamilton* played on the Public's largest stage, the Newman Theater, but the Newman has only 299 seats. That meant fewer than 36,000 seats could be sold over *Hamilton*'s entire fifteen-week run, less than the number of people who attend a single baseball game at New York's Yankee Stadium.

On the other hand, Broadway theaters typically have between 1,200 and 1,900 seats to sell for each performance. *Hamilton*'s immediate success at the Newman led producer Jeffrey Seller to think: Why not move *Hamilton* to Broadway right away? They certainly could sell more tickets, and that would earn a lot more money.

Seller was an experienced Broadway producer. He had won a Tony for producing Miranda's previous musical, *In The Heights*, and he was part of the group that decided to move another successful musical (*Rent*) to Broadway after it ran off-Broadway for only a few weeks. That decision turned out to be the right one; *Rent* went on to win the Tony for Best Musical and began what turned out to be a terrific twelve-year run.

The Tony Factor

Seller thought *Hamilton* could be another *Rent*, perhaps even greater, and he wanted to take advantage of the momentum *Hamilton* had already built. However, Seller had an even more important reason to move to Broadway as soon as possible—he wanted to compete for the 2015 Tony Awards. To do that, *Hamilton* would have to arrive at Broadway by the Tony deadline of April 23.

Seller's desire to qualify for the Tony Awards wasn't simply to attract attention and praise. It also concerned a harsh business reality: Broadway is a business, and Broadway shows are designed to make money for their investors. Winning Tony Awards could help *Hamilton* do just that.

Tourists Love Broadway

While people who live in or near New York City certainly love their Broadway shows, studies have shown that out-of-towners actually buy about two-thirds of Broadway tickets. Thousands of people come to visit New York City every week, and Broadway stages provide some of Manhattan's most popular attractions. These new theatergoers can continue to feed a Broadway show's ticket sales long after New Yorkers have already seen it.

How do out-of-towners choose their Broadway shows, often buying their tickets weeks or even months ahead of their planned visit? While reviews and word-of-mouth recommendations are certainly important, winning Tony Awards ranks at or near the top. Broadway learned long ago that winning Tonys is a great recipe for selling tickets and making money.

Not So Fast

While Seller wanted to move to Broadway right away, *Hamilton*'s creative team did not. Led by Lin-Manuel Miranda, the team felt deeply that *Hamilton* needed more fine-tuning before moving uptown to the brighter lights and larger theaters of Broadway.

After what the *New York Times* called "weeks of tense discussions," Miranda and the others convinced Seller to put off Broadway for several months. The new target date for *Hamilton*'s Broadway debut became July 2015.

Now that the moving date was settled, Miranda and his team kept working on *Hamilton* even while they performed each night at the Public. Ron Chernow reportedly saw the show more than twenty times, taking notes and making suggestions as *Hamilton* continued to take shape.

One thing the team didn't do was cut *Hamilton*'s length. Some critics suggested that the show could be even better if it ran just a bit less than its two hour and forty-five minute running time (including a fifteen-minute intermission). Miranda and his supporters quickly trashed the idea.

Asked if they believed their show could be shorter, Miranda and Kail said they were not counting the minutes but rather, "trying to find the right number of events in the story and the most compelling way to tell the story." Eustis stated his opinion more bluntly. "People who say that fifteen minutes should be cut are people who can't analyze anything other than the time on their watch."

When *Hamilton* finally made its debut on Broadway, Miranda, Kail, and Eustis proved to the world that they were right.

Smash on Broadway

With a budget of $12.5 million, *Hamilton* began its previews in Broadway's Richard Rodgers Theatre on July 13, 2015, with its official opening night scheduled for August 6. Even before its first performance at the Rodgers, *Hamilton* was a huge hit, sold out months in advance with sales already passing $32 million. An impressive list of celebrities endorsed the show, including the President of the United States, Barack Obama.

Reviewers jumped on board right from the opening curtain, lining up to sing *Hamilton*'s praises. When the CBS television program *60 Minutes* featured an interview with Miranda just before the Tonys, host Charlie Rose introduced the segment by describing *Hamilton* in glowing terms:

> Ten months ago, the Broadway musical *Hamilton* struck like a cultural earthquake, shaking up the worlds of theatre, music and American history ... The man responsible for all this is Lin-Manuel Miranda, [who] took stories from dusty history books and conjured up living, breathing human beings.

A SONG
BEYOND WORDS

Hamilton consists almost entirely of forty-six songs, and each one stands on its own merits. Some musical numbers boast rapid-fire rap lyrics and hip-hop beats; others offer catchy pop melodies or traditional Broadway ballad styles. Joy, sorrow, anger, frustration, grief—nearly every *Hamilton* song stirs up a strong emotional reaction.

When reviewers give their take on a new Broadway musical, they often anoint one musical number as the "show stopper," that one most memorable song that defines the play and brings the audience to its feet.

So … which *Hamilton* song qualifies as the "best?"

While everyone agrees that *Hamilton* follows Broadway tradition— by offering a show stopper during every performance—no one agrees on which song should carry that title.

Media reviews and online articles all offer their own choices for *Hamilton*'s most powerful song. For some, "My Shot" stands out as Alexander Hamilton's call to action. For others, it's "The Room Where It Happens," in which Aaron Burr expresses his frustration on being left out of a back-room deal between Hamilton and James Madison. Or "What'd I Miss?," Thomas Jefferson's jazz-influenced, bouncy introduction after he returns from his years in France.

Equally popular choices include "You'll Be Back," British King George III's witty breakup song to his American colonies. Or "Burn," Eliza Hamilton's searing cry of sadness and anger when she learns of her husband's betrayal. Or "Helpless," a cheerily catchy musical testament to love. Or any number of others.

Some people see another clear choice. *Hamilton* contains nearly 24,000 words, yet perhaps the most powerful song in the play begins with the lyrics:

> There are moments that the words don't reach,
> There is suffering too terrible to name.

Miranda had been struggling to write a song that described how Eliza Hamilton reconciled with her husband Alexander while they both grieved after their son Philip was killed in a duel. Miranda could not find the words to express the emotions he knew that Alexander and Eliza would be feeling, and then it came to him: there *were* no words, and the song should say exactly that. Once he got that first line, Miranda wrote "It's Quiet Uptown," a song of grief and forgiveness, in just one day.

Miranda and Jeremy McCarter later remembered that, "Actors cried while singing it, the production team cried while listening to it, Andy [Blankenbuehler] couldn't bear to choreograph it." Many audience members react the same way.

According to the *Huffington Post*, "*Hamilton* is not just a retelling of revolutionary acts. It is revolutionary."

And The Winner Is ...

On February 15, 2016, *Hamilton* made history as the first Broadway show to perform on the Grammy Awards live via satellite from Broadway when the cast performed the opening number, "Alexander Hamilton." *Hamilton* went on to win a Grammy that evening for Best Musical Theater Album for its platinum-selling Broadway cast recording.

Then, the awards parade began in earnest. On April 18, 2016, *Hamilton* won the Pulitzer Prize for Drama. Just weeks later, on May 3, *Hamilton* was nominated for a record-breaking sixteen Tony Awards, with entries in every eligible category and multiple nominations for Best Actor

BROADWAY'S FASTEST SONG
In "Guns and Ships," the actor who plays the Marquis de Lafayette performs one of the fastest-tempo songs in Broadway history. At one point, he must sing nineteen words in just three seconds.

and Best Supporting Actor. On May 20, *Hamilton* won outstanding production of a Broadway or off-Broadway musical at the Drama League Awards, where Miranda also won the evening's distinguished performance award.

Finally, on June 12, 2016, *Hamilton* dominated the Tony Awards with eleven wins, including the evening's top honor, Best Musical.

Sold out for months in advance, universal accolades, record-breaking awards... *Hamilton* certainly was doing it all. So, what exactly was it that made—and makes—*Hamilton* so special?

Miranda's Unique Take

First and foremost, *Hamilton* held on to its rap and hip-hop roots even as it transformed from a concept music album to a Broadway musical.

Some observers hailed *Hamilton* as the first major musical featuring hip-hop, but that's not really true. Russell Simmons's *Def Poetry Jam* ran for six months on Broadway more than ten years earlier; a show named *Bring in 'da Noise, Bring in 'da Funk* featured rap and tap-dancing even earlier than that. In fact, Miranda himself combined hip-hop and rap with Latin rhythms when he wrote the music and lyrics for his previous show *In the Heights*.

Hamilton, however, took rap to a new level. Miranda told Charlie Rose that rap was "uniquely suited to tell Hamilton's story, because it has more words per measure than any other musical genre." The use of rap helps Miranda pack more than 20,000 words into a two-and-a-half hour run time—roughly 144 words per minute, according to Leah Libresco at *FiveThirtyEight*. "If *Hamilton* were sung at the pace of the other Broadway shows I looked at, it would take four to six hours," Libresco wrote. She found that the musical's fastest-paced verse, from the song "Guns and Ships," clocked in at 6.3 words per second.

Creative History

Rap's ability to pack in the information was important to Miranda because he wanted to "get the history right" while making a two-hundred-year-old story come to life in modern terms.

For example, Miranda stages a debate between Alexander Hamilton and Thomas Jefferson as a modern-day, urban, rap battle. "Battle rapping incorporates a lot of elements; moving the crowd, flipping your opponent's insults, verbal prowess," Miranda explains, "but the stakes are rarely as high as the direction your country takes. I wanted to write battle raps with exactly those stakes in mind ... The fun in writing these debates is of course articulating the perspectives of these men in a way that feels contemporary."

Some find it hard to believe that a Broadway musical can use rap songs and clever rhymes to explain such complex subjects as the creation of a national bank and a "dinner deal" that moved the capital of the United States south from New York City to Washington, DC. *Hamilton* manages to do that in ways that help today's young people relate more closely to issues that faced the Founding Fathers.

FACTS ABOUT *HAMILTON*

Run Dates (including previews)

Public Theater (off-Broadway): January 20, 2015–May 3, 2015

Richard Rodgers Theatre (Broadway): July 13, 2015–present*

PrivateBank Theatre (Chicago): September 27, 2016–present*

National US tour: March 10, 2017–present*

Gross Sales

Broadway: Approximately $3 million per week;
$156 million per year (projected for 2017)

Number of Performances (including premieres)

Broadway: 904*

Awards (categories won)

2015: Lucille Lortel (10), Outer Critics Circle (3), Drama Desk
(8), New York Drama Critics Circle (1), Off Broadway Alliance (1),
Theatre World (1), Obie (1)

2016: Tony (11, including Best Musical, Book of a Musical, Original
Score, Actor in a Musical, Featured Actor in a Musical, Featured
Actress in a Musical, Costume Design of a Musical, Lighting
Design of a Musical, Direction of a Musical, Choreography and
Orchestrations); Drama League (2), Pulitzer (Drama), Grammy (1),
Broadway.com Audience (10)

*As of mid-September 2017.

Tribute to Hip-Hop Artists

Given Miranda's expert use of rap and hip-hop to tell his historical story, it seems fitting that he filled *Hamilton* with references to famous hip-hop and rap artists he admired.

In the song "My Shot," Alexander Hamilton describes himself as "Only nineteen but my mind is older," nearly an exact quote from hip-hop duo Mobb Deep and what Miranda describes as their "greatest lyric." He credits artists Big Pun and Busta Rhymes for rap techniques he uses in the show, and *Hamilton* also references other artists such as the Fugees, Grandmaster Flash, Brand Nubian, and the Notorious B.I.G.

Beyond rap and hip hop, one of *Hamilton*'s magical surprises is that, contrary to what many people expect in advance, Miranda's forty-six songs offer a wide mix of musical styles. Alisa Solomon, reviewing the show for the *Nation*, wrote:

> Thanks to the arrangements by musical director Alex Lacamoire, the score includes tinkling harpsichords, schmaltzy strings, and lush choral harmonies. The Schuyler sisters ... trade fast-talking verses and harmonize on choruses in an R&B groove that sounds like Destiny's Child; [Aaron] Burr ... busts out with a fit of envy in the form of a razzmatazz show-tune, "The Room Where It Happens." Thomas Jefferson ... opens the second act returning from Paris and asking, in a boogie-woogie number, "What'd I Miss?" ...

England's King George pouts about the loss of the colonies in the mode of a bouncy British breakup tune. …

Echoing Broadway's Past

Hamilton shows it's more than hip-hop in another way: Miranda doesn't just pay homage to hip-hop artists he admired; he does the same for traditional Broadway.

Miranda grew up listening to Broadway musicals, and he admits modeling parts of *Hamilton* after favorite shows including *Jesus Christ Superstar* and *Les Misérables*. He also adapts specific lines from other famous musicals for his own characters, such as when Aaron Burr uses a line from *South Pacific* about racism ("You've got to be carefully taught") during a debate about slavery and equality. Alert listeners can pick up references to other musicals as well, including *The Pirates of Penzance*, *A Funny Thing Happened on the Way to the Forum*, and *1776*.

New York Then and Now

While *Hamilton*'s music evokes the sounds of twenty-first-century city streets, its action takes place in eighteenth-century New York. Miranda and the rest of the *Hamilton* creative team wanted to make sure that the look and feel of their play immersed the audience in both time periods.

That was a tall order. Paul Tazewell (costumes), Andy Blankenbuehler (choreography), and David Korins (set design) worked closely with other team members not only to get the history right, but to create the right mood as well. While Miranda's music and lyrics certainly qualified as innovative, Tazewell, Blankenbuehler, and Korins each made unique contributions to *Hamilton*'s success.

With twenty years of Broadway experience, Tazewell had designed costumes for shows set well in the past (*The Color Purple, Doctor Zhivago*) and today (*Magic/Bird, In the Heights*). When he heard Miranda's demos, he knew that *Hamilton* would need to somehow combine both ideas. "The challenge was figuring out where those two eras meet, and what percentage of this world is hip-hop and what percentage is eighteenth century," he says. Tazewell combined his knowledge of current street fashions with what he saw in paintings from Hamilton's time to come up with a look that he described as "Period from the neck down, modern from the neck up."

Old and New Moves

Blankenbuehler also knew that he needed to combine the past and the present in his choreography, so he mixed elements of hip-hop dance with traces of 1940s dancer Gene Kelly and modern-day Justin Timberlake. Blankenbuehler devised a language he calls "stylized heightened gesture," which included everything from the way a chair is moved to how the cast takes their bows at the curtain call. "Other choreographers build portraits," said Stephanie Klemons, dance captain and associate choreographer. "Andy's experience is like a 3D IMAX fresco."

After listening to many of Miranda's demo songs, set designer David Korins also knew that he couldn't possibly depict all of the show's scenes. The action occurs in too many locations, and scenes shift too quickly from one place to another. Korins's scenery needed to appeal to the audience's imagination rather than draw an accurate picture.

Tazewell, Blankenbuehler, and Korins all received Tony nominations. Blankenbuehler and Tazewell went on to collect two of *Hamilton*'s eleven wins.

Diversity the Key

While most of the characters in *Hamilton* are based on white historical figures, the actors and actresses who play them hail from all races and backgrounds. Miranda envisioned a diverse cast for *Hamilton* right from the first moment he imagined turning Ron Chernow's biography into a hip-hop mixtape.

Miranda told the *New York Times*:

> Our goal was: this is a story about America then, told by America now, and we want to eliminate any distance—our story should look the way our country looks. Then we found the best people to embody these parts. I think it's a very powerful statement without having to be a statement.

Hamilton's revolutionary mixture of hip-hop and diversity quickly became one of its most highly praised qualities. Blogger Kendra James wrote that *Hamilton* allows "younger students who hear or see this musical … to start drawing connections between Miranda's revolutionary *Hamilton* and current events." The MacArthur Foundation noted that "Melding a love of the musical with a pop culture sensibility, Miranda is expanding the conventions of mainstream theater and showcasing the cultural riches of the American urban panorama." Cast member Leslie Odom Jr. said that, "When I think about what it would mean to me as a thirteen-, fourteen-year-old kid, to get this album or see this show— it can make me very emotional."

Some Questions

While most praised *Hamilton*'s diverse collection of great performers, some did wonder why the original casting call used language seeking out "non-white actors." Miranda explained that this was simply a way to include a diverse cast when non-white actors may have thought that a play about the Founding Fathers would exclude them.

"It's inclusive language," Miranda said. "It's 'I know this is about the Founding Fathers, but there's work for you here!' The reality is, we've always had white ensemble members. That's always been a part of the show. The idea has always been to look the way America looks now, and that doesn't exclude anyone."

Miranda noted that they later slightly revised the language "to make sure everyone knew that we have never turned anyone away from auditioning for our show. That was just never the case. That being said, this is a story where I think the diversity of what's on stage is essential to its success."

Great reviews, sold-out performances, and record-breaking awards certainly support *Hamilton*'s reputation as one of the most impressive musicals of all time. Few could have imagined, however, that *Hamilton*'s influence would extend far beyond Broadway and impact American society itself.

A TURN TOWARDS SUCCESS

David Korins had worked with many of the *Hamilton* team members before, including Lin-Manuel Miranda, Tommy Kail, Alex Lacamoire, and Andy Blankenbuehler. Yet, in order to get the job as *Hamilton*'s set designer, he had to go on an interview.

Korins had heard that Miranda was working on a musical based on Ron Chernow's book. Knowing the team and that the approach would likely be groundbreaking, Korins reached out to pitch the job of set designer. "Really, no one knew what it would be," he said in the *Huffington Post*. "It wasn't like, 'I want to try to hook onto this juggernaut.' It was just like, 'these are my friends! These are my guys.'"

When he was contacted for an interview, Korins took the opportunity very seriously. He did a lot of research and visited historical sites in New York, including the Morris-Jumel Mansion, which served as one of Washington's headquarters during the Revolutionary War. He outlined every scene and sketched out many ideas. He also borrowed a line from the play during his interview when he said 'I'm not throwing away my shot. You've got to hire me.'"

Korins's stage includes numerous ropes and pulleys, as well as staircases that move and walls that change location and grow larger. It's all very impressive, but what strikes everyone the most is the turntable.

Hamilton's set includes a double turntable, a rotating circle at center stage, framed by scaffolding and a catwalk to help the audience imagine the ships that carried immigrants to America. Korins mentioned the idea of constructing a turntable to Kail during their first meeting, suggesting that a spinning floor could add energy and motion to the action. "You can move people magically," he said. Kail did not like the idea at first, but Korins kept at it, and Kail later agreed.

Korins says he drew inspiration for the turntable's design from the US Capitol Building's round dome, which he then imagined as split in half, its support beams exposed. The revolving turntable contributes to the feeling that the characters and action continuously swirl around the stage. The turntable also turned out to be an essential element during the scene where Alexander Hamilton and Aaron Burr confront one another.

As Ben Brantley wrote in the *New York Times*, "The use of a revolving stage in a set has seldom seemed more apt; this world never stops spinning."

Chapter 4

Hamilton: Building A Legend

O n November 2, 2015, President Barack Obama attended *Hamilton* on Broadway during a special fund-raising event. When the audience saw the President enter, they stood and gave a loud, extended ovation. After the applause ended, President Obama skillfully quoted a song title from the play by asking the crowd, "What'd I miss?"

It's difficult to live in New York City and miss anything about *Hamilton*. Its move to Broadway sparked such excitement that city residents were treated to a fireworks display over the Hudson River on opening night. The first shell hurtled into the sky at precisely 10:45 p.m. on

Opposite: President Barack Obama talks with the cast and crew after attending Hamilton in July 2015.

August 6, 2015, just as the cast ended its performance at the Richard Rodgers Theatre.

Since that night, the buzz and excitement over *Hamilton* has not ended. If anything, it's grown even greater. The most recent block of tickets for the Broadway production, good for performances from March 6, 2017 through August 19 of the following year—2018—nearly sold out as soon as they hit the market. The show continues to break box office records, with ticket sales alone topping the $3 million mark each week.

What makes *Hamilton* so special?

What A Show

First and foremost, *Hamilton* is simply an amazing work of art. Music, lyrics, set design, choreography, lighting, sound—*Hamilton* hits all the high notes, as its haul at the Tony Awards attests.

Hamilton's first few moments draw audience members to the front of their seats as they try to absorb all the information thrown their way, delivered in rap cadence during "Alexander Hamilton," the opening number. And that's just the beginning.

Over the next two hours and forty-five minutes, theatergoers experience the full range of emotions, from laughter to tears to sheer awe, as *Hamilton*'s story unfolds. As the cast takes its final bow, many in the crowd vow to come back or buy the cast album; they also become passionate advocates, begging everyone they know to see the show for themselves so they can share the experience.

Entertaining, to be sure. But, for many people, *Hamilton* operates on even higher levels not usually reached by other Broadway musicals.

Living History

Lin-Manuel Miranda admired Ron Chernow's book because it avoided the typically dry, just-the-facts descriptions used in most history texts. Chernow painted Alexander Hamilton and other historical figures in broad, colorful strokes that revealed their humanity; they felt the same emotions, doubts, and fears as anyone else. Miranda approached *Hamilton* in much the same way.

Miranda has said:

> Every play or work of fiction kind of has to start with you identifying a character and saying, "I know this guy. I could write that guy." And I kind of ran with that. I think we take great pains to knock these guys off their pedestals. This is Washington impatient and yelling … This is Jefferson and Hamilton squabbling. These guys didn't get tablets in stone from a mountaintop. They compromised. They made mistakes … And I think it's an important reminder that they are as human as us.

Miranda's approach strikes a chord with most who see the show, including members of the cast. Leslie Odom Jr. said, "He made these dead white guys make sense to a bunch of black and brown people. He's made them make sense in the context of our time, with our music." For Daveed Diggs, *Hamilton* gave him something he did not have before, ownership of his own history. "This is the only time I've ever felt particularly American, is in the last … eight months that I've been working on this," he said in 2016.

Connection to Today

Miranda has said that one of the interesting things about the play is that the arguments between characters are the same ones that politicians wage today: "I think what's fun and resonant … is that the battles that Hamilton and Jefferson had that really created our two-party system are the battles that we're still having," Miranda said. "We're always going to be having those fights— they're part of the fabric of our creation."

It's clear that *Hamilton*'s success has fanned new interest in the Founding Fathers. Chernow certainly appreciates that; sales for his biography *Alexander Hamilton* spiked upward after *Hamilton* premiered, returning the book to the *New York Times* bestseller list many years after it was first published.

While previous musicals had already brought hip-hop to Broadway, those shows featured music directly related to the theme of the play. For example, *In the Heights* told the story of a diverse uptown neighborhood by using characters who looked and sounded like they lived there.

Hamilton broke that Broadway mold by retelling an old story in today's language, using contemporary music and diverse twenty-first-century casting. Jeremy McCarter always thought hip-hop would work on Broadway regardless of the show's topic; Miranda proved him to be right.

Leading Women

Miranda liked something else about Chernow's book: it included strong women. Chernow paid a lot of attention to the two main women in Hamilton's life, Angelica Schuyler and Eliza Schuyler Hamilton. Miranda did the same, writing powerful songs for each so they could tell their own stories.

Renée Elise Goldsberry, who played Angelica in the original cast, said, "One of the things that's exciting to me about playing Angelica Schuyler, and feeling so powerful … is that we get to show who the founding mothers are, and what they did, and they were not just sewing flags."

Diversity and Access

Hamilton changed the face of the Tony Awards and of Broadway itself. In 2016, fourteen of the available forty performance nominations went to actors of color, seven of them to *Hamilton* cast members. Their success has encouraged many other performers, writers, musicians, and designers of all races and backgrounds to believe that Broadway's path to glory may now be open for them as well.

On another front, *Hamilton*'s extensive use of social media set a totally new tone for plays and musicals. Even people who cannot get tickets can now watch online videos of actual performances both on and off the Richard Rodgers Theatre stage. Fans can easily link to social media sites and get news about the play and its performers, helping the *Hamilton* team to build relationships far beyond the stage.

Taking It on the Road

Hamilton's breathtaking success convinced producer Jeffrey Seller and the team that it was time to spread the joy beyond New York City. That would be a daunting task; Seller wanted to make sure that new versions would be just as good as the Broadway original.

The first road production of *Hamilton* began its previews on September 27, 2016, at the PrivateBank Theatre in Chicago before officially opening on October 19. Chicago loves *Hamilton* just as much as New York does. The Chicago run was extended once as of mid-September 2017, through April 2018.

A second company of *Hamilton* began a limited California run when it started previews in San Francisco at the Orpheum Theatre on March 10, 2017 and opened on March 23. That show ended August 5 so it could move to the Pantages Theatre in Los Angeles, where it first previewed on August 11 and opened five days later. The Los Angeles production was set to run through December 2017.

The *Hamilton* team then announced that a second national tour would start in early 2018, beginning in San Diego, California in January and making its way to sixteen other cities through the rest of the year. Plans to visit more cities in 2018 and 2019 are in the works, and the first international opening was scheduled for London, United Kingdom, on December 21, 2017.

Tough Ticket

Many people want to see *Hamilton* but, in reality, few actually can. Seating is limited; even the Richard Rodgers Theatre offers just a few more than 1,300 seats for each performance. In reality, more than twice as many people can attend one football game than can see *Hamilton* in a month!

The combination of few tickets and high demand leads to another problem: the price for Broadway shows has skyrocketed. The box office currently sells most *Hamilton* seats for between $179 and $199, although two hundred premium seats run $849 each. However, all seats sell out almost immediately; resellers then offer seats to the public for $1,000, $2,000 or more—each!

To try to address the high cost, the *Hamilton* team dusted off an idea that Jeffrey Seller had used years earlier for *Rent*. They set up a lottery: each night forty-six seats would be sold for $10 each. As soon as the lottery was announced, crowds began to line up outside the Richard Rodgers Theatre, hoping for their chance to see the show that everyone was talking about.

After seeing the lines, some cast members from *Hamilton* and other musicals decided to take their skills to the sidewalk and perform short, fun shows to entertain the crowd. Miranda himself took part in some of what came to be known as the #Ham4Ham shows. Miranda said he did so because he knew that most people who line up for the lottery won't win, and he didn't want them to walk away with nothing.

The lottery proved to be so popular that it moved online to avoid crowding city streets and endangering fans, and *Hamilton* has now expanded the lottery to its other cities as well.

New Blood

As *Hamilton*'s Broadway run extended past its first anniversary, members of the original cast came to realize that it was time for them to move on to other projects.

On July 9, 2016, Lin-Manuel Miranda, Leslie Odom, Jr., and Phillipa Soo performed for the final time at the Richard Rodgers Theatre. Daveed Diggs soon followed, ending his run on July 15; Renée Elise Goldsberry left on September 3. Jonathan Groff, who took over the role of King George III when the production moved to Broadway, had already left the show in April.

Despite the cast changes, *Hamilton* continues to motor on, consistently exploring new and creative ways to attract new fans.

In October 2015, the people behind *Hamilton* took an important additional step to move beyond the Broadway stage and make a real difference in people's lives. They decided to create a program to help teachers bring American history to the classroom in a new way.

The Hamilton Education Project later expanded to include Chicago and San Francisco. On April 26, 2017, more than five thousand students and teachers attended matinee performances of *Hamilton* across all three cities. Plans for 2017–2018 include introducing the program to still more locations as *Hamilton* tours the United States.

SONG TO REMEMBER
Miranda wrote the melody to "The Story of Tonight" when he was sixteen and singing in a band with his friends. He remembered it as a song shared among young friends dreaming of the future.

Talking about the program, Miranda said, "I do believe firmly that approaching history in this way [...] forces you to reckon with what you're going to do with your life. And I think it forces you to confront what it is to live a life of meaning [...] whether that's theater or whether that's architecture or whether that's medicine or biology."

Miranda also likes the effect of having young people in the audience. Miranda told *Rolling Stone*:

> The student matinees are when you learn the truth. Young people haven't learned theater etiquette yet ... when someone gets shot, they go, "Ohhhhh!" The rap battles, they light up. This very dense, historically accurate musical makes these people come alive in their heads ... I think we have a unique opportunity for people who feel like musicals aren't for them to say, "This is for you."

Records, Tapes, Books, and Film

Hamilton's magic has extended well beyond the New York stage and its national tour. The *Hamilton* original Broadway

INTO THE CLASSROOM

During *Hamilton*'s run at the Public Theater, Ron Chernow invited Lesley S. Herrmann of the Gilder Lehrman Institute of American History to see the show. Gilder Lehrman has a long track record of supporting programs that help schools to teach history. As soon as the play finished, Herrmann turned to Chernow and said, "We have to get this in the hands of kids."

Miranda already knew how powerful the experience of creating your own artistic project could be for young people. The first musical he ever wrote was for a class assignment. Seller also believed in connecting art with education; he had already introduced Broadway to high school students through a program he developed for the musical *Rent*.

Seller and Luis Miranda, Lin-Manuel's father, recruited the Rockefeller Foundation to donate $1.5 million to help fund what became the Hamilton Education Program and pay for tickets for twenty thousand students. *Hamilton* offered each seat for $70, its cost without any profit. The Rockefeller Foundation then contributed $60 while students paid only $10.

Before students saw the show, teachers introduced them to the people, events, and documents of that time. Students also learned how Lin-Manuel Miranda used primary sources to help him do research and how they could use sources to produce their own original performances. The program encouraged students to be creative and portray the history of the Founding Fathers in their own way. They could choose what people or events to include, and they could rap, recite poetry, sing, dance—whatever form of expression they could think of.

The project also provided guides for the classroom and a website with links to primary sources to help students find information. Videos included *Hamilton* clips as well as interviews with Miranda, other cast members, and Ron Chernow.

Teachers and students alike love the program. For many history teachers, making "old" subjects come alive stands out as their biggest challenge. "This has just given us a cool factor," said Justin Emrich, an Ohio social studies teacher. Moses Ojeda, principal of the Thomas Edison School in Jamaica, Queens, called it a game-changer and reported that students showed much more interest in American history after participating.

Sixteen-year-old Pedro de Los Angeles, a Harlem student in upper Manhattan, told *Newsweek* that "It just stuck in my head, and I found history interesting. If history class was like that every day, I'm pretty sure [exams] wouldn't be a problem."

cast recording, which includes all forty-six songs from the show, was released in September 2015. It became the first Broadway musical to win the Billboard Music Award for Top Soundtrack/Cast Album, and it won the 2016 Grammy Award for Best Musical Theatre Album. It also peaked at number one on the Rap Album chart, the first cast album ever to do so. As of March 2017, it had sold more than three million copies.

Miranda also fulfilled his original vision when he released *The Hamilton Mixtape* in December 2016. The recording's twenty-three selections include remixes, originals, and songs that Miranda did not include in *Hamilton*, performed by artists including The Roots, John Legend, and Kelly Clarkson. The *Mixtape* has also been widely successful, debuting at number one on the Billboard 200.

Hamilton's story has also been put on film. In 2009, Miranda played a demo of the song "Alexander Hamilton" for filmmaker Alex Horwitz. Horwitz realized even then that Miranda was on the path to creating something special, and he decided to film a record of the project from its earliest stages to its triumph on Broadway. *Hamilton's America*, his documentary, premiered on PBS on October 21, 2016.

What's Next

Miranda has stayed busy since leaving the cast. Among his many projects, he collaborated on writing the music for the Disney film *Moana*, he hosted *Saturday Night Live*, and he will soon be starring in the *Mary Poppins* film sequel *Mary Poppins Returns*. A year after *Hamilton* dominated the Tony

Awards, Miranda returned to the Tony stage to present the 2017 award for Best Musical to *Dear Evan Hansen*.

While Miranda and other cast members have moved on, *Hamilton*'s story continues to unfold in ways that further confirm its influence beyond Broadway.

In fact, *Hamilton*'s success may have saved Alexander Hamilton's place on the $10 bill. The US Treasury had considered removing Hamilton in favor of a famous American woman. However, in April 2016, the Treasury announced that it instead planned to replace Andrew Jackson on the $20 bill with abolitionist Harriet Tubman, due at least in part to the attention *Hamilton* attracted to its namesake's valuable place in history. Replacing Jackson with Tubman was not a certainty after the elections of November 2016, but Hamilton's place is safe.

It's also reported that the musical's success even caused prices to rise for homes and apartments in Hamilton Heights, the neighborhood near Alexander Hamilton's former home (now a National Park Service site) in modern-day Harlem in upper Manhattan. And, in true Broadway tradition, *Hamilton* inspired its own parody; the off-Broadway spoof *Spamilton* both pokes fun at, and celebrates, the famous musical.

In 2016, Miranda and McCarter published their own book. *Hamilton: The Revolution* includes Miranda's thoughts about how his musical came into shape and his notes about songs and characters in the play. Miranda and McCarter wrote their book because they wanted the story behind *Hamilton*'s creation to be told and remembered.

A Story Told

Eliza Hamilton devoted the final fifty years of her life trying to tell her husband's story, yet Alexander Hamilton never received the attention or respect that other Founding Fathers commanded. Ron Chernow helped to correct that wrong in his award-winning biography.

A few years later, Miranda provided another new perspective on Hamilton and how his story would be remembered. In *Hamilton*'s final scene, Alexander Hamilton takes Eliza's hand and leads her to the front of the stage as the cast sings a question to the audience:

"Who tells your story?"

As the final notes end and a silence falls across the theatre, the answer to that question becomes clear: Miranda just told Hamilton's story, in perhaps the most powerful and imaginative way possible.

Then, with thunderous applause and a standing ovation, the audience joins with Miranda and the *Hamilton* team, committed to spreading the word.

In 2016, *Hamilton* received sixteen Tony Award nominations, the most for a musical in Broadway history, including two for Best Actor (Lin-Manuel Miranda and Leslie Odom, Jr.) and three for Best Featured Actor (Daveed Diggs, Christopher Jackson, and Jonathan Groff). Eleven *Hamilton* team members walked away with the top prize in their category; only 2001's *The Producers* managed to win more Tony awards (it won twelve).

RANK	TITLE	YEAR	NONIMATIONS	AWARDS WON
1	Hamilton	2016	16	11
2	The Producers	2001	15	12
3	Billy Elliot: The Musical	2009	14	10
4	The Book of Mormon	2011	14	9
5	Company	1971	14	6
6	Spamalot	2005	14	3
7 (tie)	Dreamgirls	1982	13	6
7 (tie)	The Drowsy Chaperone	2006	13	5
7 (tie)	Hairspray	2003	13	8
7 (tie)	In the Heights	2008	13	4
7 (tie)	Kinky Boots	2013	13	6
7 (tie)	Me and My Girl	1987	13	3
7 (tie)	Ragtime	1998	13	4

Glossary

ACT The main sections or divisions of a musical or play.

BIOGRAPHY The written story of someone else's life.

BOX OFFICE The location that sells tickets to a performance, usually located at the theater itself. It also refers to the amount of tickets sold for a performance in dollars.

BROADWAY The largest and most famous theater district in New York City, which encompasses theaters with more than five hundred seats located close to Broadway, a long street in Manhattan.

CAST The people who perform in a show.

CASTING CALL An invitation for performers to apply for a role in a media production.

CHOREOGRAPHER The person who creates dances and arranges movements for a musical.

DEMOS Sample recordings of music sent to someone to raise interest.

DIALOGUE The words that are spoken in a play.

DIRECTOR The person who coordinates how a show is presented by working with the actors and actresses and arranging staging.

DRAMATIC LICENSE An artist's freedom to create a work based on the artist's interpretation rather than strictly following the facts.

DUEL A prearranged combat between two people fought with deadly weapons according to accepted rules.

GRAMMY AWARDS Awards presented by the National Academy of Recording Arts and Sciences for musical recordings.

IMPROV Improvising, or performing without preparing specific parts in advance.

INTERMISSION The pause or break between acts of a play or musical, usually lasting for approximately fifteen minutes.

LYRICS The words of a song.

MATINEE An afternoon performance of a show.

OFF-BROADWAY A term used to describe smaller New York City theaters, usually holding 99 to 499 seats.

OPENING NIGHT The first official performance of a play or musical in its final form.

OPTIONED Arranging for the right to use someone else's literary work to make a play or movie based on the same subject.

PREVIEW Public performances of plays or musicals that help the director make changes and judge audience reaction before the show officially opens.

PRODUCER The person responsible for managing all areas of a musical, play, film or TV show, including hiring cast and crew and arranging financial support.

RUN The number of times a show is performed.

SET DESIGNER The person who designs the sets and scenery for a show.

TONY AWARDS Awards given each year for excellence in live Broadway theater.

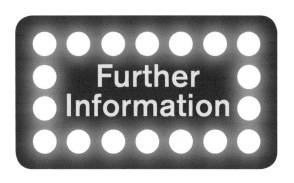

BOOKS

Chernow, Ron. *Alexander Hamilton*. New York: Penguin Books, 2005.

Miranda, Lin-Manuel, and Jeremy McCarter. *Hamilton: The Revolution*. New York: Grand Central Publishing, 2016.

WEBSITES

About The Hamilton Education Program

https://www.gilderlehrman.org/programs-exhibitions/about-hamilton-education-program

Hamilton—The Official Site

http://www.hamiltonbroadway.com

Hamilton's official website contains information about the play's background and future plans, as well as videos from the play and other social appearances and events beyond the stage. It also includes links to the details regarding *Hamilton* performances in New York, Chicago, London, and on the National Tour.

Lin-Manuel Miranda—The Official Website

http://www.linmanuel.com

Find out everything you want to know about Lin-Manuel Miranda, the genius behind *Hamilton*, including his biography, awards, his music, other projects and the latest news, as well as how to link to him on social media.

This website from the Gilder Lehrman Institute describes the Hamilton Education Program and includes links to information about Alexander Hamilton.

The Official Page For The
Music of Hamilton: The Musical

http://atlanticrecords.com/HamiltonMusic

Atlantic Records provides information about the musical and the Mixtape. The site lists all of *Hamilton*'s forty-six songs; click on a song title and you can see all the lyrics as well as listen to a short sample of that song.

CDS

Hamilton (Original Broadway Cast Recording). New
York: Atlantic Records Group, 2015. Available on CD,
downloads and through streaming services.

VIDEOS

Lin-Manuel Miranda Performs at the White House Poetry Jam

https://www.youtube.com/watch?v=WNFf7nMIGnE

Writer and star of the Broadway musical *Hamilton*, Lin-Manuel Miranda performs the first song he wrote for his concept album "The Hamilton Mixtape" at the White House Evening of Poetry, Music, and the Spoken Word on May 12, 2009. The song became the opening number to the musical *Hamilton*.

The origins of the revolutionary musical "Hamilton"

https://www.cbsnews.com/videos/the-origins-of-the-revolutionary-musical-hamilton

This CBS News video from June 12, 2016, gives a five-minute report on the play, its origins, and its original cast with interviews, scenes and songs from the play.

70th Annual Tony Awards 'Hamilton'

https://www.youtube.com/watch?v=b5VqyCQV1Tg

The original *Hamilton* cast performs at the 2016 Tony Awards, with a filmed introduction by President Barack and First Lady Michelle Obama.

Bibliography

WEBSITES

"Alexander Hamilton." Biography.com, April 27, 2017. https://www.biography.com/people/alexander-hamilton-9326481.

Binelli, Mark. "'Hamilton' Creator Lin-Manuel Miranda: The *Rolling Stone* Interview." *Rolling Stone*, June 1, 2016. http://www.rollingstone.com/music/features/hamilton-creator-lin-manuel-miranda-the-rolling-stone-interview-20160601.

"Broadway sensation 'Hamilton' hits bookshelves." CBS News.com, April 12, 2016. https://www.cbsnews.com/news/creators-of-broadway-hip-hop-musical-hamilton-release-book.

Brooks, Katherine. "11 Things Every Die-Hard 'Hamilton' Fan Wants You To Know." *Huffington Post*, January 31, 2017. http://www.huffingtonpost.com/entry/hamilton-musical-fans_us_56c34d45e4b0c3c55052a5cd.

——— "Step Inside The World Of 'Hamilton,' A Spectacular Stage You Might Never See." *Huffington Post*, June 8, 2016. http://www.huffingtonpost.com/entry/hamilton-set-design-interview_us_5757ffd8e4b0a3d6fbd3362a.

——— "100,000 Students Across The U.S. Will Probably See 'Hamilton' Before You Do." *Huffington Post*, June 27, 2016. http://www.huffingtonpost.com/entry/ hamilton-musical-eduham-porgram-expanding_ us_576c29c0e4b0aa4dc3d4c7b5.

Carra, Mallory. "How Historically Accurate Is 'Hamilton'? A Breakdown Of The Musical's Events & What Really Happened So Long Ago." Bustle.com, June 12, 2016. https://www.bustle.com/articles/165821-how-historically-accurate-is-hamilton-a-breakdown-of-the-musicals-events-what-really-happened-so.

Davenport, Ken. "What Does A Broadway Producer Do? Over 100 Producers Respond." *The Producer's Perspective*, accessed September 14, 2017. https://www.theproducersperspective.com/my_weblog/2010/05/what-does-a-broadway-producer-do-over-100-producers-respond.html.

Delman, Edward. "How Lin-Manuel Miranda Shapes History." *Atlantic*, September 29, 2015. https://www.theatlantic.com/entertainment/archive/2015/09/lin-manuel-miranda-hamilton/408019.

Flanagan, Linda. "How Teachers Are Using 'Hamilton' the Musical in the Classroom." KQED.org, March 14, 2016. https://ww2.kqed.org/mindshift/2016/03/14/how-teachers-are-using-hamilton-the-musical-in-the-classroom.

Gerard, Jeremy. "'Hamilton' By The Numbers: Anatomy of A Broadway Blockbuster." *Deadline*, September 18, 2015. http://deadline.com/2015/09/hamilton-by-the-numbers-anatomy-of-a-broadway-blockbuster-1201534240.

———— "Review: 'Hamilton's Revolution Still Shoots Fireworks Over Broadway." *Deadline*, June 25, 2017. http://deadline.com/2017/06/review-hamilton-broadway-revisit-1202119694.

Green, Adam. "Lin-Manuel Miranda's Groundbreaking Hip-Hop Musical, *Hamilton*, Hits Broadway." *Vogue*. June 24, 2015. http://www.vogue.com/article/hamilton-hip-hop-musical-broadway.

"HAMILTON: A HISTORY." LinManuel.com, accessed September 4, 2017. http://www.linmanuel.com/hamilton.

"The Hamilton Mixtape." Genius, accessed September 5, 2017. https://genius.com/albums/Lin-manuel-miranda/The-hamilton-mixtape.

"Hamilton segment on 60 Minutes." Vimeo, accessed September 5, 2017. https://vimeo.com/179969954.

"HAMILTON'S Celebrated Education Program Makes History Today." *Broadway World*, April 26, 2017. https://www.broadwayworld.com/article/HAMILTONs-Celebrated-Education-Program-Makes-History-Today-20170426.

Healy, Patrick. "'Hamilton' Will Get Broadway Stage." *New York Times*, February 24, 2015. https://www.nytimes.com/2015/02/25/theater/hamilton-will-not-rush-to-broadway.html?mcubz=0&_r=0.

Houck, Jeanne. "Theater: Hamilton." *American Historian*, accessed September 6, 2017. http://tah.oah.org/february-2016/theater-hamilton.

Leopold, Todd. "Why We Love 'Hamilton'." CNN, February 12, 2016. http://www.cnn.com/2016/02/12/entertainment/hamilton-musical-grammys-feat/index.html.

Light, Alan, and Greg Tate. "Hip-hop: Music and Cultural Movement." Encyclopedia Britannica, June 29, 2016. https://www.britannica.com/topic/hip-hop.

McCarthy, Erin. "20 Things You Might Not Have Known About *Hamilton.*" *Mental Floss*, November 17, 2015. http://mentalfloss.com/article/71222/20-things-you-might-not-have-known-about-hamilton.

McPhate, Mike. "California Today: 'Hamilton' Sweeps Through the State." *NYTimes.com*, August 16, 2017. https://www.nytimes.com/2017/08/16/us/california-today-hamilton-los-angeles.html.

"Most Tony nominations ever: How does 'Hamilton' stack up to history?" *Los Angeles Times*, May 3, 2016. http://www.latimes.com/entertainment/arts/culture/la-et-cm-tony-most-nominations-20160502-snap-htmlstory.html.

O'Falt, Chris. "'Hamilton's America': Behind the Scenes of Documenting Lin-Manuel Miranda's Hit Musical." *IndieWire*, September 20, 2016. http://www.indiewire.com/2016/09/hamilton-america-documentary-lin-manuel-miranda-alex-horwitz-pbs-nyff-documentary-1201728621.

Paulson, Michael. "Hamilton Heads to Broadway in a Hip-Hop Retelling." *New York Times*, July 12, 2015. https://www.nytimes.com/2015/07/13/theater/hamilton-heads-to-broadway-in-a-hip-hop-retelling.html?_r=1.

Paulson, Michael, and David Gelles. "'Hamilton' Inc.: The Path to a Billion Dollar Broadway Show." *New York Times*, June 8, 2016. https://www.nytimes.com/2016/06/12/theater/hamilton-inc-the-path-to-a-billion-dollar-show.html.

"Ron Chernow: Pulitzer Prize-winning author of *Washington: A Life* and *Alexander Hamilton*." Penguin Random House Speakers Bureau, accessed September 8, 2017. https://www.prhspeakers.com/speaker/ron-chernow.

Rubino-Finn, Olivia. "Broadway Budgets 101: Breaking Down the Production Budget." *New Musical Theatre*, January 22, 2016. http://newmusicaltheatre.com/greenroom/2016/01/broadway-budgets-101-breaking-down-the-production-budget.

Runcie, Charlotte. "What is Hamilton? A 12-step guide to your new musical obsession." *Telegraph*, January 30, 2017. http://www.telegraph.co.uk/theatre/what-to-see/what-is-hamilton-a-12-step-guide-to-your-new-musical-obsession.

Schama, Simon. "Simon Schama on Broadway show 'Hamilton'." *Financial Times*, June 3, 2016. https://www.ft.com/content/762ea27a-2815-11e6-8b18-91555f2f4fde.

Schuessler, Jennifer. "'Hamilton' and History: Are They in Sync?" *New York Times*, April 10, 2016. https://www.nytimes.com/2016/04/11/theater/hamilton-and-history-are-they-in-sync.html?_r=0.

Seymour, Lee. "'Hamilton' Leads Broadway's Highest Grossing Season Ever." *Forbes*, May 23, 2017. https://www.forbes.com/sites/leeseymour/2017/05/23/hamilton-leads-broadways-highest-grossing-season-ever-for-2016-2017/#7468988d6381.

"60 Minutes Presents: A Front-Row Seat." *CBS News*, February 5, 2017. https://www.cbsnews.com/news/60-minutes-presents-a-front-row-seat.

Sokolove, Michael. "The C.E.O. of 'Hamilton' Inc." *New York Times Magazine*, April 5, 2016.https://www.nytimes.com/2016/04/10/magazine/the-ceo-of-hamilton-inc.html?mcubz=0&_r=0.

Solomon, Alisa. "How 'Hamilton' Is Revolutionizing the Broadway Musical." *Nation*, August 27, 2015. https://www.thenation.com/article/how-hamilton-is-revolutionizing-the-broadway-musical.

Soloski, Alexis. " Sixteen ways Hamilton transformed theater – and the world." *Guardian*, May 3, 2016. https://www.theguardian.com/stage/2016/may/03/hamilton-tony-awards-broadway-lin-manuel-miranda.

Strauss, Valerie. "The unusual way Broadway's 'Hamilton' is teaching U.S. history to kids." *Washington Post*, June 28, 2016. https://www.washingtonpost.com/news/answer-sheet/wp/2016/06/28/the-unusual-way-broadways-hamilton-is-teaching-american-history-to-kids/?utm_term=.ec150060a2ec.

Weller, Chris. "'Hamilton' is the most important musical of our time." *Business Insider*, March 19, 2016. http://www.businessinsider.com/hamilton-is-the-most-important-musical-of-all-time-2016-3.

Vozick-Levinson, Simon. "Revolution on Broadway: Inside Hip-Hop History Musical 'Hamilton'." *Rolling Stone*, August 6, 2015. http://www.rollingstone.com/culture/features/revolution-on-broadway-inside-hip-hop-history-musical-hamilton-20150806.

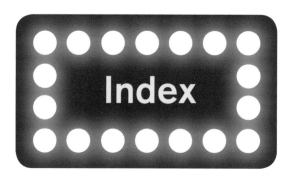

Index

About the Author

GERRY BOEHME is a published author, editor, speaker, and business consultant who lives in New York. Gerry has written books for students dealing with many subjects and especially enjoys talking with people who have different backgrounds and opinions. Gerry purchased tickets to see *Hamilton* more than one year in advance and says, "It was well worth the wait."